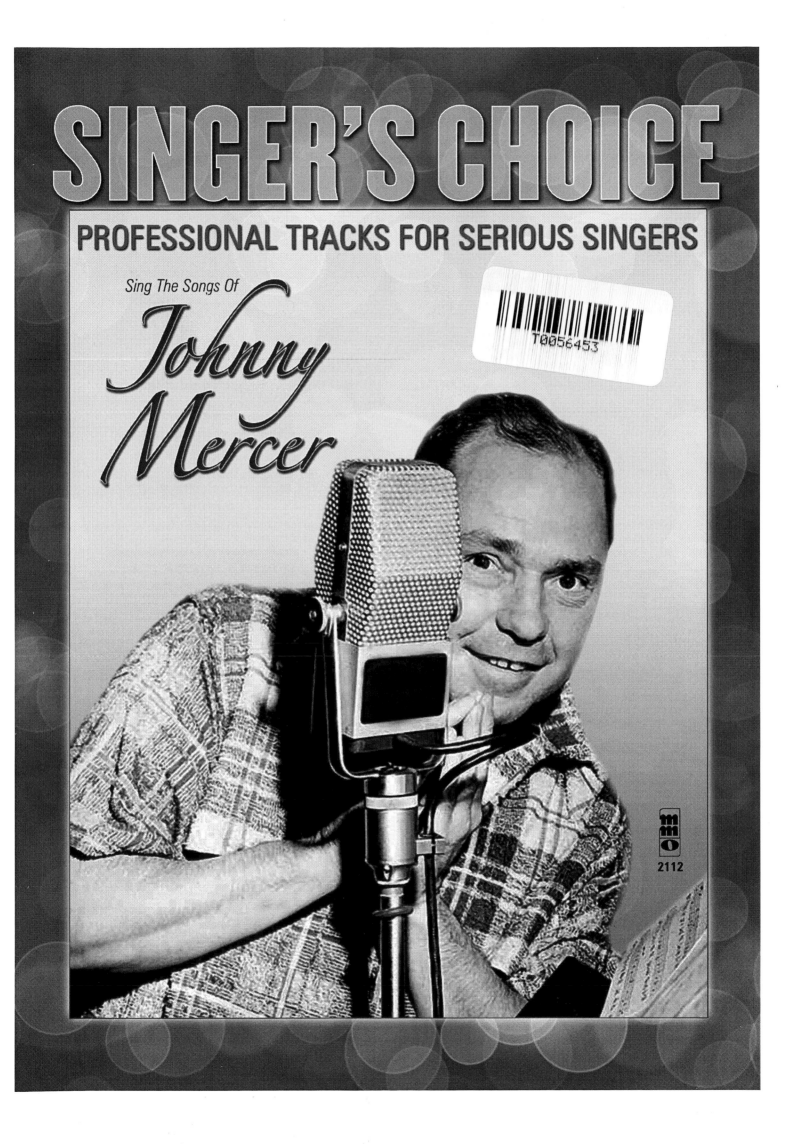

SINGER'S CHOICE

PROFESSIONAL TRACKS FOR SERIOUS SINGERS

Sing The Songs Of

Johnny Mercer

T0056453

MMO
2112

- notes continued from back cover

Johnny Mercer had his first successes in 1932 with "Pardon My Southern Accent" and especially "Lady Bones" which he wrote with Hoagy Carmichael. In 1935 Mercer returned to Hollywood to write songs and occasionally act in RKO musicals. He appeared in a couple of forgettable movies (Old Man Rhythm and To Beat The Band) and collaborated with Fred Astaire on "I'm Building Up To An Awful Let-Down." After writing "I'm An Old Cowhand From The Rio Grande" for Bing Crosby in 1936, he became in great demand as a lyricist, giving up his attempts to be an actor.

From that point on, Mercer had hit after hit. Among his most popular songs from the second half of the 1930s were "Goody Goody," "Too Marvelous For Words" (written with Richard Whiting), "Hooray For Hollywood," "Jeepers Creepers," and "You Must Have Been A Beautiful Baby." During that period he also wrote "Day In, Day Out" and "Fools Rush In," the latter a ballad favorite for male singers heard with swing orchestras. Mercer also penned the words to an instrumental by trumpeter Ziggy Elman that became "And The Angels Sing."

Johnny Mercer did not neglect his singing career, appearing regularly on the radio in 1939 with the Benny Goodman big band. While Mercer collaborated with many songwriters during his career, he and Harold Arlen were an ideal team. They both had backgrounds in jazz and were familiar with the blues, coming together to create such sophisticated standards as "Blues In The Night," "My Shining Hour" (from the movie of the same name), "One For My Baby," "That Old Black Magic" and "Come Rain Or Come Shine" during 1941-46. Some of his most personal lyrics were written for "I Remember You" which was composed after the breakup of his love affair with Judy Garland.

Mercer also continued to work on an occasional basis with Hoagy Carmichael, having great success with 1941's "Skylark" (a song recorded by a countless number of performers) and 1951's "In The Cool, Cool, Cool Of The Evening." Mercer had a mid-1940s hit with "On The Atchison, Topeka and the Santa Fe." "Tangerine" was an early 1940s hit for Jimmy Dorsey and "Mr. Meadowlark" was also popular during the later years of the swing era. Mercer also wrote lyrics for songs that had already caught on including "Laura," "Midnight Sun," "Autumn Leaves" and "Satin Doll"; his words made the tunes even bigger hits.

In 1942, Johnny Mercer co-founded Capitol Records with fellow songwriter Buddy DeSylva and record store owner Glen Wallichs. Mercer soon helped sign such artists as Nat King Cole, Stan Kenton and Jo Stafford to the new label, and recorded vocal hits of his own for several years.

The rise of rock and roll in the mid-1950s may have slowed down Johnny Mercer's output a bit but he continued to write classic lyrics, writing for films and Broadway shows. His later works included "Moon River," "Days Of Wine And Roses" and "Charade" (all three written with Henry Mancini). As late as 1974, Johnny Mercer recorded two albums of his songs.

In 1975 Paul McCartney showed interest in collaborating with Mercer but unfortunately the lyricist was already very ill. Johnny Mercer passed away in 1976 at the age of 66. Even after his death, there were more Johnny Mercer songs. Some of his lyrics were discovered and Barry Manilow was hired to write the music, resulting in several interesting ballads including "When October Goes."

Johnny Mercer's words are timeless and still sound topical and inventive today.

– Scott Yanow,
author of 11 books including Swing,
Jazz On Film and Jazz On Record 1917-76

Sing The Songs Of

Johnny Mercer

CONTENTS

ISBN 978-1-941566-13-8

4

Autumn Leaves

Words and Music by
Johnny Mercer and Joseph Kosma

Fools Rush In

Words and Music by
Johnny Mercer and Rube Bloom

MMO 2112

I Remember You

My Shining Hour

Words and Music by
Johnny Mercer and Harold Arlen

Skylark

Words and Music by
Johnny Mercer and Hoagy Carmichael

Tangerine

Words and Music by
Johnny Mercer and Victor Schertzinger

Too Marvelous For Words

Words and Music by
Johnny Mercer and Richard Whiting

Mr. Meadowlark

Words and Music by
Johnny Mercer and Walter Donaldson

Music Minus One

50 Executive Boulevard • Elmsford, New York 10523-1325

914-592-1188 • e-mail: info@musicminusone.com

www.musicminusone.com

MMO 2112

ISBN 978-1-941566-13-8